A Prophecy for America: Broken Pledge, Broken Covenant

By E.A. Windischman

TKP Press
The Kingdom Paradigm, LLC

ISBN-13: 978-0-9973731-1-0
ISBN-10: 0-9973731-1-0
Library of Congress Control Number: 2021909100

© 2021 By E.A. Windischman

The Kingdom Paradigm, LLC
Woodridge, IL

The Bible text designated KJV is from the 1769 *Authorized Version*, commonly known as the *King James Version*.

Scripture marked NKJV is taken from the *New King James Version®*. Copyright © 1982 by Thomas Nelson. Used by permission. All rights reserved.

This work is licensed under the Creative Commons Attribution-NonCommercial-NoDerivatives 4.0 International License. To view a copy of this license, visit http://creativecommons.org/licenses/by-nc-nd/4.0/.

The text of this work may be reproduced and shared under the terms of the above license for non-commercial purposes.

Contents

CONTENTS	2
DEDICATION	3
THE PLEDGE OF ALLEGIANCE	4
ONE NATION UNDER GOD	8
THE BROKEN COVENANT	12
THE CALLING	14
MESSAGES FOR THE AMERICAN NATIONS	17
The "Church" of Falsehood	20
The Church of Truth	22
The People of Israel	24
For the Native American Tribes	27
To those who Follow Islam	29
To the Followers of Hinduism	31
Canada	33
Mexico	34
WARNING FOR AMERICA	35
Poverty, Famine, Fire, and War	39
For the Faithful Bride:	41
A FINAL REFLECTION	43
ENDNOTES	47

Dedication

Dedicated to the Lord of all Creation who guided the Pilgrim Fathers to the new world where liberty and justice could be established.

Chapter 1

THE PLEDGE OF ALLEGIANCE

"I pledge allegiance to the Flag of the United States of America, and to the Republic for which it stands, one Nation under God, indivisible, with liberty and justice for all."

Something is happening to the United States of America. Something sinister is afoot, yet at the same time hope remains that somehow the sinister signs we see all around us might not mean total doom. What is this sinister move and what are the signs that point to it? And is there reason for hope? America like the mythical phoenix can rise again from judgment, but only if we return to God. I pray that we have ears to hear.

The Pledge of Allegiance made it's appearance in 1892 just over 100 years into our Constitutional Republic.[1] The pledge reflects the core principles upon which this nation was built to aspire to: Unity, Liberty, and Justice for all. Even, or should I say especially, the phrase "one Nation under God", for it is the outworking of this aspiration that gives rise to the Unity, Liberty and Justice for all.

While they were the last words to be added to the Pledge under President Eisenhower in 1954, the phrase "one Nation under God" reflects the earliest aspirations of those who contributed to the founding of this nation, and rightly belongs in a pledge to our republic. From the Native American's devotion toward the "Great Spirit", the earliest European settlers from Columbus to the pilgrims[2], through the great awakenings, revivals, and mission movements, the longing to acknowledge and be of service to our Creator was in hearts of many if not most of the citizens of this nation.

 So, what is happening to this country? What is happening to the core principles on which this country was founded? The great divide and hatred seen in our political landscape is only a symptom of a much deeper malady. Left, Right, Democrat, Republican, Independent, Green, whatever: this sinister sickness stems from the abandonment of our Pledge of Allegiance to the flag and the Republic for which it stands. We are no longer "One Nation under God" because the nation as a people and their political establishment has forsaken God, and forsaken the principles of "Liberty and Justice for all" which can only come from seeking and obeying God. **In the breaking of the Pledge of Allegiance citizens have recited from their youth, we have broken the covenant our founders made with God and with each other**.

Chapter 2

ONE NATION UNDER GOD

It should come as no mystery that while multiple motives can be ascribed to the various early settlers, a core conviction of many settlers was to seek a better life though the freedom to worship God according to conscience. One group of settlers in particular, aka the "pilgrims" as they called themselves, came over on the Mayflower carrying the spirit of liberty and a conviction to bring glory to God.[3] The text of the "Mayflower Compact" follows.[4] Signed in 1620 by all adult passengers of the Mayflower, it is considered a precursor to the principles of liberty and participatory self-government outlined in the "Declaration of Independence". Many early State constitutions, the "Articles of Confederation" and the "US Constitution", especially the first 10 Amendments know as the "Bill of Rights" all build on the early foundations of self government established in the Mayflower Compact.[5] My emphasis is in "**bold**".

In the name of God, Amen. We whose names are underwritten, the loyal subjects of our dread sovereign lord King James, by the grace of God, of Great Britain, France, and Ireland King, Defender of the Faith, etc.

*Having undertaken, **for the glory of God**, and **advancement of the Christian faith**, and honor of our king and country, a voyage to plant the first colony in the northern parts of Virginia, **do** by these presents solemnly and mutually in the presence of God and one of another, **covenant** and combine ourselves together into a civil body politic, for our better ordering and preservation, and furtherance of the ends aforesaid; and by virtue hereof to enact,* *constitute, and frame such just and equal laws, ordinances, acts, constitutions, offices from time to time, as shall be thought most meet and convenient for the general good of the colony: unto which we promise all due submission and obedience. In witness whereof we have hereunder subscribed our names; Cape Cod, the 11th of November, in the year of the reign of our sovereign lord King James, of England, France and Ireland eighteenth and of Scotland fifty-fourth, Anno Domini 1620.*

The "**bold**" was added to emphasize these three elements of their undertaking:
   1) For the Glory of God
   2) For the Advancement of the Christian faith
   3) The establishment of a "Covenant" between themselves and God

Just to clarify, a "covenant" is a solemn, legal, and sacred agreement people enter into between themselves, with God, or with all three. That is why we use "covenant" to describe the marriage agreement; "covenant" is the term that describes the agreement God made with Israel through Moses. The "new covenant" is the agreement God made with the people Israel (commonly identified as Jews today) and members of all other nations who come to faith in Jesus the Messiah. This "new covenant" was inaugurated by Jesus during the Passover meal (last supper) and sealed by his crucifixion and resurrection. "The Christian faith", as it is commonly known, is actually the fulfillment of numerous promises God made to and through the people of Israel (i.e. see the book of Jeremiah 31:31). Therefore, the term Judeo-Christian describes the general faith principles of our founding, and our culture, even if each individual does not adhere to these principles.

In light of the above, to form their "civil body politic" the Mayflower settlers were to frame "just and equal laws, ordinances, acts, constitutions, offices from time to time, as shall be thought most meet and convenient for the general good of the colony: unto which we promise all due submission and obedience". In other words, **they agreed to the rule of law, under the authority of God, in agreement with one another for their mutual benefit**.

Chapter 3

THE BROKEN COVENANT

In today's America, over a period of time a great number of laws and practices in society have arisen which are not to "the glory of God", nor are they "just and equal", but in reality just the opposite: dishonoring to God, unjust and biased. Unjust laws, unjust and ungodly judges, and ungodly trends in the lifestyles of our citizens leading away from the God of our forefathers; these are the national, societal, and individual sins that represent a breaking of the covenant our founders made between one another and with God. The country is breaking the pledge we have said from our youth. All this leads to the erosion of our liberty, because true liberty can only come from God.

The broken pledge and broken covenant has led to the extreme divisiveness we see today. **If left un-rectified, the broken covenant will lead to the dissolution of the nation and bring the judgment, if not the wrath, of Almighty God for this nation's sins**. At this point I am not even sure these sins need to be defined, but because our society's conscience has become seared and calloused, and because justice demands that the accused knows the accusations against him or her, we will bring to the forefront the core sins of the nation. We take as our coach the Biblical prophet Amos, and encourage you, the reader of this indictment against America, to read Amos as he makes God's case against the northern kingdom of Israel and its surrounding nations, including the kingdom Judah. The LORD said through Amos:

> ***"Surely the Lord GOD does nothing, Unless He reveals His secret to His servants the prophets."* (Amos 3:7, NKJV)**

Chapter 4

THE CALLING

In the book of Amos, we first get an introduction to Amos himself. He was a "herdsman, aka sheep breeder" (Amos 1:1,7:14), and also tended Sycamore trees for their fig fruit. When confronted by a corrupt priest named Amaziah, the lackey of a corrupt political leader (king) who wanted him to get lost, Amos said this:

"I was no prophet, nor was I a son of a prophet, but I was a sheep breeder and a tender of sycamore fruit. Then the LORD took me as I followed the flock, and the LORD said to me, 'Go,

prophesy to my people Israel.'" (Amos 7:14-15 NKJV)

Amos was just an imperfect guy trying to make an honest living, but likely was grieved at what he saw happening in society around him, so God called him to speak out. In the same manner, believe me I am an imperfect guy yet trying to make an honest living, and I also am grieved at the deep backsliding our nation is under; it is certain there will be those who will want me to get lost as well. It would be dishonest to say that God has not been speaking to my heart, as I know he has been speaking to the hearts of multitudes of his people and patriots in our country about the evil that is taking place right before our eyes. God is saying to his people:

"Go, prophesy to America, a land of milk and honey whose people and leaders have abandoned and broken their covenant with me. Call them to repentance and I may lighten some of the severe judgments that her sins have called for. For I will not entirely relent, as the river rises and effects all who dwell on its banks, so my judgments will effect all, but my people who seek my face and know my name I will not forsake."

Chapter 5

MESSAGES for the AMERICAN NATIONS

Amos was also instructed to deliver messages to the surrounding nations. His indictments were phrased with "for three transgressions and for four" etc. This figure

of speech was not to give an exact count of transgressions, but was a way of saying that there is more than enough to warrant the pronouncements being given.

America's closest neighbors are Canada and Mexico and as the Lord speaks to individuals, families, tribes, regions, cities, governments, nations and the world, he has messages for our neighbors to the north and south. Additionally, in America there are internally, while citizens, those who still carry a separate identity among themselves: the several Native American tribes or "nations", the people of Israel (the Jewish people), Muslim citizens who believe in the establishment of an "Islamic State", various other ethnicities, and even the "Church" as an institutional establishment and as a "people" of God. We do not use the term "race", because according to the Bible, there is only one race, and that is the human race (Genesis 1:27-28; 9:1,19; Acts 17:26).

All Americans need to embrace, at least hear and understand, the founding principles that are the source of the freedoms that people come to the United States to experience. These principles are outlined in the 10 words of the covenant from Sinai; the standards of a just and free society commonly know as the 10 Commandments; and the good news of God's salvation and forgiveness of sin found in Jesus Christ. The nation needs to understand that the gift of liberty is from God, and we owe God our allegiance because of it. Is this not what the Exodus of Israel from Egypt exemplified, being set free and then pledging loyalty and allegiance to the One who set us free and to follow His just principles of social life? The gift of freedom God graced to America demands the same.

The "Church" of Falsehood

To the "church of falsehood" in America, for judgment begins at the house of God, the Holy Spirit is saying:

"For three transgressions and for four am I bringing judgment on those who use the term "church" to describe themselves. For you deny my name and flout in my face your disregard for my holy word. Your synods, conferences and councils are repulsive to me where you choose the world and reject me. You participate in the sins of Sodom, have I not said that "outside are dogs", but you allow sexual confusion and rebellion to remain in your camps, and even embrace it. Because of you the world is trapped in darkness, when you claim to give light. The masks you wear represent the muzzles you have placed on my word. I Jesus declare that you have rejected me, and the cup you drink is the cup of damnation. Drink deep of your cup, for the poison will run through your veins, as your conscience is seared, so will be your bodies in the day of judgment when you join the Devil and his angels in the eternal fire."

The Church of Truth

To my Church that still believes and knows that I AM the Way, the Truth and the Life, clinging to every word that proceeds out of the mouth of God, the Spirit of Christ says:

"My Church is built on me, says the ROCK, the Holy One of Israel. My Church is  built on the Holy Spirit and Fire. My Church is built on the Word of God and the Power of God. My Church is built on the foundation of the Apostles and Prophets, but many have built upon the foundation wood, hay and stubble...this will burn.

Build, my people, build upon the truth of my teaching from the beginning until the end. Be a family, be a people, be my bride, not a dead institution with dead programs. Build upon Moses, the Psalms, and the Prophets. Build upon the Good News that I Jesus came to fulfill them and have made a New Covenant with the House of Israel and with the House of Judah, a covenant that invites all people and nations, all the children of Adam, to enter into my grace through my death on the cross and the power of my resurrection, to be born anew and become my children.

Do not hold back, declare, proclaim, and disciple until the very end. For those that endure to the end shall see my kingdom established in the earth. Knowledge of the LORD shall cover the earth as the waters cover the sea."

The People of Israel

To the people of Israel and the House of Judah who share in the citizenship of America the Holy One of Israel says:

"For three transgressions and for four am I bringing judgment on those who have been called by my name of old, but not to the extent of that which I will bring judgment on the "church of falsehood".

In your synagogues you read but do not hear, you hear but do not understand. Many have embraced the ways of the deceiver. Some of this I permitted until the nations had their chance to enter the new covenant, but now the time has come for Israel to return to me as I have returned many to the land I promised them.

Call upon me and I will answer, declare, "Blessed is He who comes in the name of the LORD". It is time to reject the ways of the world, the ways of Globalism, the "New World Order", the ways of so called liberalism; these are the ways of Belial; these are the ways of a false faith and a pretended people. They are the ways of Babel, not the ways Zion. Instead embrace me, the one who shed his blood on the altar of atonement for you.

Embrace your destiny and calling to be a light to the nations, be blessed and be a blessing. Unite with those of the nations who have come to know me, and share with them your deep roots in Abraham, roots that have their life in the Messiah, the Holy one of Israel, Yeshua your Salvation. Only this faith can save you as anti-Semitism is rising and you will need the power and authority that comes from embracing your Savior, and the alliance and fellowship of those whom I have called from all nations to serve me and be my children.

To those who know me and those who will, as I warned through my servant John, the dragon will make war with the offspring of Israel who keep the commandments of God and have the testimony of Jesus the Messiah. Make sure you are on the right side of this war says the LORD."

For the Native American Tribes

To the Native Americans the Great Spirit says:

"For three transgressions and for four I have brought, and am bringing judgment upon the nations that have rejected me, you will share in the judgment on America, but your tribes can also experience a greater rebirth, like water in the desert, and rain in the wilderness.

As has been true among all nations and peoples that were outside of Israel, whom I allowed to go their own way for a time to worship demons and imaginations of their own hearts, yet I preserved ancient roots of truth that could be awaken your spirit when my gospel was proclaimed. This is true of the entire world, from Africa to Europe, India, China, and the Islands of the seas. Your various tribes and nations have been and are no exception.

Many of you have embraced my gospel, even from the earliest of days when your ancestors first heard the message of the cross, and many elements of your culture, outside of the demon worship that some still cling to, have enriched all the people of America and even the world. But many have refused to embrace the true path to freedom, the true path to spiritual awakening that is only found in the One who shed his blood for all, who was born of and now truly sends "the Great Spirit" to fill the hearts of those who trust in Him.

He who created all that is, in the world you see and in the world you cannot is calling you to repent and embrace the Truth, for I am the Way, the Truth, and the Life, says Jesus your Savior."

To those who Follow Islam

To Muslims upon America's shores the King of Kings, the Son of God would say:

"For three transgressions and for four you will share in my judgment: Why seek an Islamic State? Why seek a state of slavery and submission to error propagated by one who refused to understand who I am and what I did for all mankind.

Your book acknowledges my virgin birth, my miracles, my supernatural presence beyond any human, but denies the most important work, my death on the cross for your sins and my resurrection. But I am revealing myself to those who have been lost in the lies they have been told from their youth.

Many of you have come to America for the freedoms offered, but have chosen to remain as slaves to error. Your alliance in this world to Marxism and dictatorship will reap bitter rewards in the end for all who do not repent.

Your zeal has been impressive, but zeal for lies and error leads to destruction. Use your freedom now to come to know the one you call the prophet Isa, in truth Yasue al Masih. I am the way to eternal life, only in my love can you escape the damnation of hell your sins and the rejection of the truth have earned you."

To the Followers of Hinduism

To the Hindu people in America the one true God would say:

"For three transgressions and for four will you share in the judgments I bring upon the land you have made your  home: You bring a system of beliefs from the East taught by ancient principalities and powers, spiritual wickedness in heavenly places.

You have a form of spirituality, but not of my Spirit, not of my Power, and not of my Truth. I Jesus have come to set the captives free from the lies of deceptive spirits.

You have many books and many legends, many Veda's and many tails with shadows of truth; illusions of peace, but you don't know the Good News.

You seek for "truth" but don't know THE TRUTH. I have promised that those who seek me will find me when they search for me with all their hearts. Seek for the one and only Creator, and you will find me in the writings of the prophets of Israel and the New Testament when you search for me with all your heart, then you will be renewed in my love."

Canada

To the nation of Canada the Lord God of Israel says:

"Nations that have known me, and known my name, when they reject me, I warn with various signs of nature, but the final judgment will be invasion by wicked nations. It is time for my remnant in Canada to stand up strong and bold, for your nation along with Europe precedes the United States in wickedness and in judgment. Perhaps your country can be spared some of the severity."

Mexico

To Mexico the LORD is saying:

"You have been under judgment for some time, but you have a chance to shine says the LORD. Because of my people in your  country, you can shake off the shackles of political corruption and Marxism. It will seem like one day, in an instant, and I will break the hold of the cartels, I will break the demonic hold of corruption, and loose the power of my gospel in your midst says the Lord."

Chapter 6

WARNING for AMERICA

To the United States of America, hear the word of the LORD:

"Like a piece of pottery is broken, so is the covenant that once kept you strong and under my protection says the Spirit of Liberty. The covenant your forefathers made; to work for my glory, promote the gospel, and establish just laws, is broken. For three transgressions and for four your judgment is certain.

For the removal of my name and law from your gates and the public square, from your schools and from your markets, from your city halls and courts and federal offices.

For the shedding of innocent blood across your country through abortion, and for letting those who shed that blood go unpunished.

For allowing murderers to go free, when my law calls for murders to pay the ultimate price in order to answer the cry of innocent blood from the earth.

For corrupt judges from the highest court in the land to the lowest, who render corrupt rulings to benefit themselves when they know full well the truth and know to do right, but do not do it.

For embracing wickedness instead of righteousness, perversion instead of holiness, confusion instead of truth you have earned my judgment, and if not for those who cry out for revival and grace, my wrath.

For lethargy and complacency in those who knew and know better but allow these things to happen. For citizens who shun their rights and forsake the responsibly to be sovereign and help govern their country, you will lose your freedom and become slaves to tyranny.

For ongoing slander against one another, against me, and libel against my people in your media, newspapers, and technical conglomerates ... Have I not said, "you shall not bear false witness against your neighbor"? But your lies are as endless as your wickedness is evil.

In much the same way as I loved Israel have I loved you America, not because you were perfect, but because you at least had a heart to seek after me. Your heart has become stone toward me, your institutions utterly corrupt, and your vision dark. I offer life, but you have embraced death. You would surrender your freedom and liberty to global powers you do not know nor understand.

I have sent warnings of nature: of fire, and storm, drought. I have even allowed terror. You have not heeded the warnings, so you will not escape the severe judgments and just consequences I have yet to allow unless you repent and renew the covenant with tears and actions.

Remove the wicked judges; remove the corrupt politicians; the Marxists, and those who seek only power, control, and the wealth of this world. Remove the godless whose final end is certain.

Renew the covenant and stand for the truth given once and for all, the Ten Commandments and the exhortation to love me and love your neighbor, and speak the truth to one another.

Don't allow your neighbors and children to corrupt and pervert themselves in silence through the sexual confusion being promoted by Satan and his followers.

Don't allow the wicked to steal the livelihood from the working poor by corrupt laws and regulations that make people wards and dependents of a corrupt governmental system.

Break up the corporate monopolies that are eroding the capabilities of independent free enterprise to bring wealth to more of the people.

Poverty, Famine, Fire, and War

Upon the cities that have become centers of godlessness and corruption I am sending poverty, famine, fire, and war: New York, Chicago, San Francisco, Los Angeles, Washington DC and others that don't repent. Upon the states that have become centers of godlessness and corruption I am sending poverty, famine, fire and war: California, New York, Illinois, Washington, Oregon and others that don't repent.

You have turned your back on God and his word; you have turned your back on truth and righteousness; you have turned your back on all that is good and embrace all that is evil. You reject justice, show favoritism for power and greed, and fight against liberty and freedom. They who do such shall eat the fruit of their planting. If you sow to the wind you will reap the whirlwind.

"America, America, God shed his grace on thee, and crowned thy good with brotherhood from sea to shining sea" but you have traded grace for judgment, you have exchanged brotherhood for tribalism, and the good for the evil. How can you escape the damnation of hell?

For breaking your covenant with the LORD, hear now my judgment America: the covenant is broken, and so is your union. Without me you have no liberty, no unity, and no nation. Your gates are open to enemies and godless traitors from within, and hostile powers from outside, and the spiritual wickedness in heavenly places that your leaders and people have invited to rule over them. These powers will reign and bring chaos wherever they are welcome, but I rule over all says the LORD, and their doom is as sure as is those who follow them.

Hear this America, REPENT, and return to me says the LORD!

For the Faithful Bride:

Hear this my people, those who call upon my name with a pure heart and weep for your people and your nation, you will not be forsaken. I will uphold you with my right hand says the LORD. Like the rising river effects all on its banks, so you too will feel my judgments on this nation, but listen to my voice and stay close to my word, care for one another and you will not be forsaken.

You must be willing to lay your lives down for the truth. Where there is famine, I can supply. Where there is war, I can bring peace. Where there is hunger, I can feed. Where there is sickness I can heal, says the LORD Jesus.

I am calling my body to renew their strength in me, to reunite as a family, to become a strong tower in the midst of the land. If the wicked will not repent, then you my people reestablish the covenant your forefathers made. You rebuild America. For many wicked will be removed in my judgment, many cities laid waste, and many righteous suffer and die under persecution, but as the wealth of the wicked is stored up for the righteous, so will resources become available for my people to rebuild this nation upon the ROCK, says the LORD.

The south will become a place to rebuild and renew, as strongholds for my name are established throughout the land.

As this age comes to an end, look for my glorious appearing, my coming with thousands upon thousands of my angels and saints, and don't stop proclaiming my Kingdom says the LORD, for I AM KING OF KINGS. The kingdoms of this world will become mine says the LORD. Just a little while longer, hang on, be strong, and press forward to the coming of a new day. I will set my foot on the mount of Olivet, and I will rule and reign from Jerusalem, and the heavenly Zion will return to earth.

Salvation is only found in me, only my blood can cleanse from sin, only faith in my resurrection can bring new life. Keep this truth in the forefront of your proclamation, for you overcome by the Blood of the Lamb and the word of your testimony. The testimony of JESUS is the Spirit of prophesy."

Chapter 7

A FINAL REFLECTION

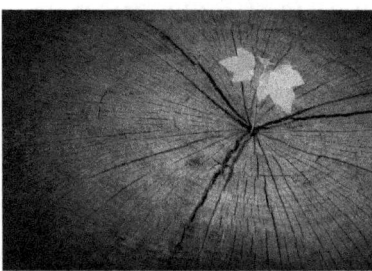

What the Lord has spoken to my heart is overwhelming. These are strong words, but meant to call America back to covenant, back to God. Not every statement is for everyone, but we must be willing to put on the shoe if it fits. It is God's kindness that leads us to repentance.

I myself am guilty of the sin of lethargy and complacency; guilty of keeping silent when I should have spoken out. Forgive me Lord. The burden is not lifted, for it is upon me to make sure the nations hear what the Lord Jesus through his Holy Spirit has shared with me. I humbly ask my brothers and sisters to help share this burden.

My brothers and sisters in the Lord are also obligated to judge what I have written and will be speaking. Some will not accept the premise that God speaks through his people today, yet God desires to speak through all his people (Nu 11:25-29, 1 Cor 14:1). My only request is that God's people judge this prophecy for America by the Holy Spirit living within them, and all God has said in His Holy Word, especially by Amos my "mentor" so to speak. Judge by what our society was, and what it has become. Judge by the signs you see around you. Judge in Spirit and in Truth, and share this message as you see fit.

    My voice is only one of many crying out, but there are still too few. It is time for the pulpits in America to return to preaching justice, judgment, and liberty. Preach the gospel in the authority of Jesus Christ and the power of the Holy Spirit. Lay down your fear, lay down your life, and take up the cross of Christ. He is calling you, he will revive your people, and they also will proclaim his word. "Perfect the saints for the work of the ministry". The ministry is not your job; it is the divine calling of all God's people.

    Elders, overseers, pastors, teachers and prophets, be finished with the "church show" and get on with training the people. You may not feel worthy, and the truth is you're not; I certainly am not. We are not worthy in ourselves, but we are the "righteousness of God in Christ Jesus" and in his righteousness and grace we must strive, not in the rags of our own righteousness.

In the opening paragraphs I ask if there is hope for America. I believe the answer is yes, but it is a hope for a new America, for the old is all but dead and the vultures are circling; the new must arise as a sprout from a cut down tree. There are a lot of fine people in this country, people who want to do what is right. But it is hard to make sense of all the mixed messages we receive every day, in addition to just carry out what we need to do to survive; keep a roof over our head and food on our table. **It is time for all the fine people in America to seek the Lord, seek Him and you will find him, and He can and will give life back to our country, and all the nations of the world that seek him in truth.** "Blessed is the nation, who's God is the LORD" (Ps 33:12).

It is also time to realize, as our founding fathers did, that those who govern do so by consent of the governed. Americans, it is time to speak up, to participate in governing your country; not just on election day, but in your schools, city counsels, town halls, and corporate board rooms. Hold the politicians who are supposed to work for you accountable. In America there should be no ruling class, no human kings, only people willing to serve. Reject life long politicians trying to take us to the cleaners and rape our land. Reject the political dynasties some have tried to establish. Stand for liberty, stand for truth, and resist tyranny at every turn. Hate the evil and love the good based on God's mandates, and we can rebuild our nation for God's glory.

    God bless those who seek after Him, and may he grant repentance and revival to America and the world before the great and glorious Day of the LORD. Jesus Christ is LORD! Amen.

Erik A. Windischman
www.thekingdomparadigm.com

Endnotes

[1] Historical facts regarding the Pledge of Allegiance, the Constitution, and other foundational documents can be found at http://www.ushistory.org ; https://usconstitution.net ; and https://www.history.com/news/who-created-the-pledge-of-allegiance .

[2] "Christopher Columbus had a mystic belief that God intended him to sail the Atlantic Ocean in order to spread Christianity. ... Columbus wrote what he called a *Book of Prophecies*, which is a compilation of passages Columbus selected from the Bible which he believed were pertinent to his mission of discovery. ... Columbus's own writings prove that he believed that God revealed His plan for the world in the Bible, the infallible Word of God. Columbus believed that he was obeying the mission God staked out for his life when he set sail west across the Atlantic Ocean."

Scott Berson, sberson@mcclatchy.com , Thomas S. Giles, christianitytoday.com , Phyllis Schlafly/Eagle Forum and Debbie Holloway, crosswalk.com "The Faith of Christopher Columbus you Don't Hear" MetroVoiceNews.com. October 13, 2019.
https://metrovoicenews.com/the-faith-of-christopher-columbus-you-dont-hear/

[3] Another very informative site is that sponsored by the Plimoth Patuxet Museums of the Plymouth Plantation, a non-prophet organization. The site commemorates the 400th anniversary of the voyage of the Mayflower.
https://plimoth.org/mayflowervoyage

[4] Facts on the "Mayflower Compact" and the text of the document quoted above are available at
https://www.britannica.com/topic/Mayflower-Compact#:~:text=Mayflower%20Compact,%20document%20signed%20on%20the%20Engl

ish%20ship,States%20of%20America.%20Pilgrims%20signing%20the%20Mayflower%20Compact

[5] A helpful article to provide a baseline of understanding can be found at The History Channel website, but I encourage every American to become familiar with our countries roots and take the time to dig deeply into the history of our founding, this link is just a brief introduction.
https://www.history.com/news/mayflower-compact-colonial-america-plymouth

May I also recommend

"The Patriot's History Reader: Essential Documents For Every American" by Schweikart, Dougherty, and Allen. Sentinel, 2011.

It contains numerous citations of source documents and brief explanatory essays to help Americans refocus on the foundations of liberty and freedom.

www.ingramcontent.com/pod-product-compliance
Lightning Source LLC
Chambersburg PA
CBHW071801040426
42446CB00012B/2654